DOG BREEDS

Cocker Spaniels

by Sara Green

Consultant:
Michael Leuthner, D.V.M.
Petcare Animal Hospital
Madison, Wisc.

BLASTOFF!
4
READERS

BELLWETHER MEDIA • MINNEAPOLIS, MN

Note to Librarians, Teachers, and Parents:

Blastoff! Readers are carefully developed by literacy experts and combine standards-based content with developmentally appropriate text.

Level 1 provides the most support through repetition of high-frequency words, light text, predictable sentence patterns, and strong visual support.

Level 2 offers early readers a bit more challenge through varied simple sentences, increased text load, and less repetition of high-frequency words.

Level 3 advances early-fluent readers toward fluency through increased text and concept load, less reliance on visuals, longer sentences, and more literary language.

Level 4 builds reading stamina by providing more text per page, increased use of punctuation, greater variation in sentence patterns, and increasingly challenging vocabulary.

Level 5 encourages children to move from "learning to read" to "reading to learn" by providing even more text, varied writing styles, and less familiar topics.

Whichever book is right for your reader, Blastoff! Readers are the perfect books to build confidence and encourage a love of reading that will last a lifetime!

This edition first published in 2011 by Bellwether Media, Inc.

Library of Congress Cataloging-in-Publication Data
Green, Sara, 1964–
Cocker spaniels / by Sara Green.
    p. cm. – (Blastoff! readers: Dog breeds)
Includes bibliographical references and index.
Summary: "Simple text and full-color photography introduce beginning readers to the characteristics of the dog breed Cocker Spaniels. Developed by literacy experts for students in kindergarten through third grade"–Provided by publisher.
ISBN 978-1-60014-457-8 (hardcover : alk. paper)
1. Cocker spaniels–Juvenile literature. I. Title.

SF429.C55G74 2010
636.752'4–dc22   2010000673

Printed in the United States of America, North Mankato, MN.

080110   1162

Contents

What Are Cocker Spaniels?

Cocker Spaniels are energetic dogs with floppy ears and long, silky **coats**. They are also called Cockers.

Cocker Spaniels are 13.5 to 15.5 inches (34 to 39 centimeters) tall and weigh 18 to 30 pounds (8 to 14 kilograms). The **breed** is a member of the **Sporting Group** of dogs.

Cocker Spaniel coats are straight or wavy. The coats come in a variety of colors. They can be **buff**, black, silver, or chocolate. Cocker Spaniels may also have **parti-color** coats.

Cocker Spaniels are born with long tails. Many owners have **veterinarians** shorten the long tail. This is called **docking** the tail.

chocolate coat

! fun fact

Buff is the most common Cocker Spaniel color.

buff coat

black coat

History of Cocker Spaniels

The **ancestors** of the Cocker Spaniel were hunting dogs called Spaniels. It is likely they came from Spain. The name "Spaniel" comes from a word that means "Spanish dog."

Spaniels were brought to England many centuries ago. They became popular hunting dogs. People used them to hunt for small animals such as birds and rabbits.

woodcock

Spaniel **litters** had puppies of different sizes. Owners chose the larger puppies to hunt pheasants and other large birds. They used the smaller puppies to hunt small birds. One such bird was the woodcock. People called the smaller dogs "Cocker Spaniels" after this bird.

! **fun fact**

A Cocker Spaniel ancestor came to the Americas on the *Mayflower* in 1620.

In the nineteenth century, people brought Cocker Spaniels from England to the United States. Americans called these dogs English Cocker Spaniels.

English Cocker Spaniel

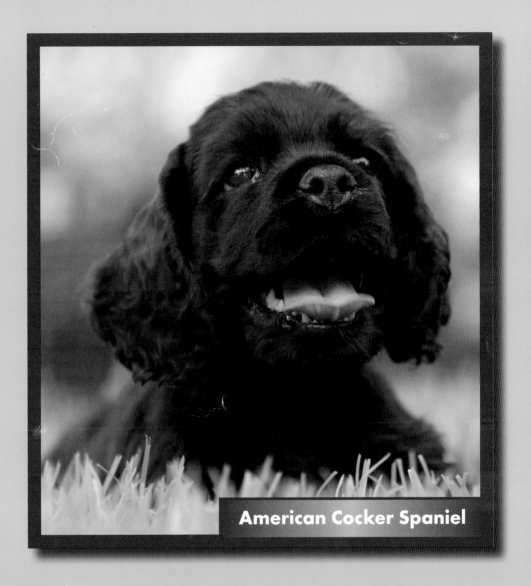

American Cocker Spaniel

American breeders chose the smallest English Cocker Spaniels to have puppies. They called these puppies American Cocker Spaniels. American Cocker Spaniels look different from English Cocker Spaniels. They are smaller and have shorter **muzzles**.

In the 1940s, breeders made the American Cocker Spaniel a separate breed. People liked the look of the breed's silky coat. The breed became a popular **companion dog**.

Today in the United States, most people call the American Cocker Spaniel by the name "Cocker Spaniel."

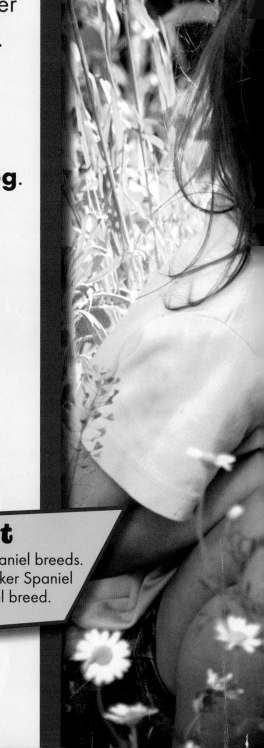

! **fun fact**

There are nine Spaniel breeds. The American Cocker Spaniel is the smallest Spaniel breed.

Cocker Spaniels Today

Cocker Spaniels are very active dogs. Many Cocker Spaniels participate with their owners in **field trials**. These trials test the dogs' skills at finding birds hidden in a field.

The dogs often cross water or walk long distances to find birds. Cocker Spaniels earn points when they **flush** birds. Cocker Spaniels with enough points earn the title of Master Hunter.

Cocker Spaniels like to run. They often participate in a sport called **agility**. An agility course has tunnels, ramps, jumps, and more.

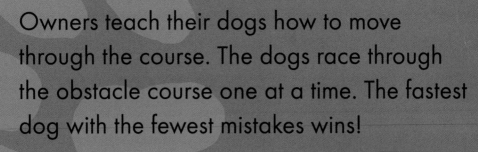

Owners teach their dogs how to move through the course. The dogs race through the obstacle course one at a time. The fastest dog with the fewest mistakes wins!

Cocker Spaniels enjoy activities on land and in water. One of their favorite games is fetch.

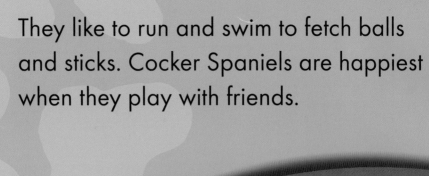

They like to run and swim to fetch balls and sticks. Cocker Spaniels are happiest when they play with friends.

Glossary

agility—a dog sport where dogs run through a series of obstacles

ancestors—family members who lived long ago

breed—a type of dog

buff—a light tan color

coats—the hair or fur of animals

companion dog—a breed of dog that provides friendship to people

docking—shortening the tail of a dog

field trials—activities where dogs test their skills at finding small animals such as birds

flush—to scare birds or small animals out from cover

litters—groups of young; puppies in a litter are born to one mother at the same time.

muzzles—the noses, jaws, and mouths of animals

parti-color—having two solid colors; one of the colors must be white.

Sporting Group—a group of dog breeds used for hunting

veterinarians—doctors who take care of animals

To Learn More

AT THE LIBRARY
American Kennel Club. *The Complete Dog Book for Kids*. New York, N.Y.: Howell Books, 1996.

MacAulay, Kelley, and Bobbie Kalman. *Cocker Spaniels*. New York, N.Y.: Crabtree Publishing, 2006.

Ramsey, Ann Louise. *Just Be You*. New Castle, Co.: Crown Peak Publications, 2006.

ON THE WEB
Learning more about Cocker Spaniels is as easy as 1, 2, 3.

1. Go to www.factsurfer.com.

2. Enter "Cocker Spaniels" into the search box.

3. Click the "Surf" button and you will see a list of related Web sites.

With factsurfer.com, finding more information is just a click away.

Index

The images in this book are reproduced through the courtesy of: Hanna Monika, front cover; Juniors Bildarchiv/Alamy, pp. 4-5; Juniors Bildarchiv, pp. 6-7; Nick Ridley/KimballStock, pp. 8, 10-11, 16-17; Jon Eppard, p. 9; Wikipedia, p. 10 (small); Andreas Gradin, p. 12; Willee Cole, p. 13; Mostovyi Sergii Igorevich, pp. 14-15; Rolf Klebsattel, p. 18; Juan Martinez, pp. 19, 20; Gary Randall/KimballStock, p. 21.